614
JON

Jones, Claire

Pollution: the
waters of the earth

DATE			
MAY 1 2 20 23			

POLLUTION:

the WATERS
of the earth

The Real World Books
on
Pollution

THE WATERS OF THE EARTH

THE AIR WE BREATHE

THE LAND WE LIVE ON

THE DANGEROUS ATOM

THE NOISE WE HEAR

THE FOOD WE EAT

THE BALANCE OF NATURE

THE POPULATION EXPLOSION

**These books are printed on
paper containing recycled fiber.**

a real world book

POLLUTION:

the WATERS
of the earth

Claire Jones
Steve J. Gadler
Paul H. Engstrom

LERNER PUBLICATIONS COMPANY
Minneapolis, Minnesota

Acknowledgments

The illustrations are reproduced through the courtesy of: pp. 6, 12, 28, 34, 38, 43 (center), 50 (top and bottom), 55, 60, 63, 64, 73, 74, 82, 91, Environmental Protection Agency, Water Quality Office; pp. 17, 23, Henry H. Valinkas; p. 19, California Department of Fish and Game; p. 24, Minnesota Department of Natural Resources; p. 32, Michigan Department of Natural Resources; p. 39, United States Department of Agriculture, Soil Conservation Service; p. 43 (top), United States Department of the Interior, Bureau of Reclamation; p. 43 (bottom), The Citizens' Advisory Committee on Environmental Quality; p. 47, Hammermill Paper Company; p. 57, C.C. Photography; p. 61, United Press International, Inc.; p. 68, Tennessee Fish and Game Commission; p. 70, California Department of Water Resources; p. 76, *Machine Design*; p. 84, Independent Picture Service.

The Library of Congress cataloged the
original printing of this title as follows:

Jones, Claire.
    Pollution: the waters of the earth [by] Claire Jones, Steve J. Gadler [and] Paul H. Engstrom. Minneapolis, Lerner Publications Co. [1970]

    95 p. illus. 23 cm. (A Real World Book)

    SUMMARY: Describes the ways in which man pollutes water resources, cites specific lakes and rivers that have become casualties of pollution, and discusses what can be or has been done to improve the situation.

    1. Water—Pollution—Juvenile literature. [1. Water—Pollution] I. Gadler, Steve J., joint author. II. Engstrom, Paul H., joint author. III. Title.

TD422.J65   333.9'1   77-156363
ISBN 0-8225-0627-0   MARC
                                                   AC

International Standard Book Number: 0-8225-0627-0
Library of Congress Catalog Card Number: 77-156363

Fourth Printing 1977

Contents

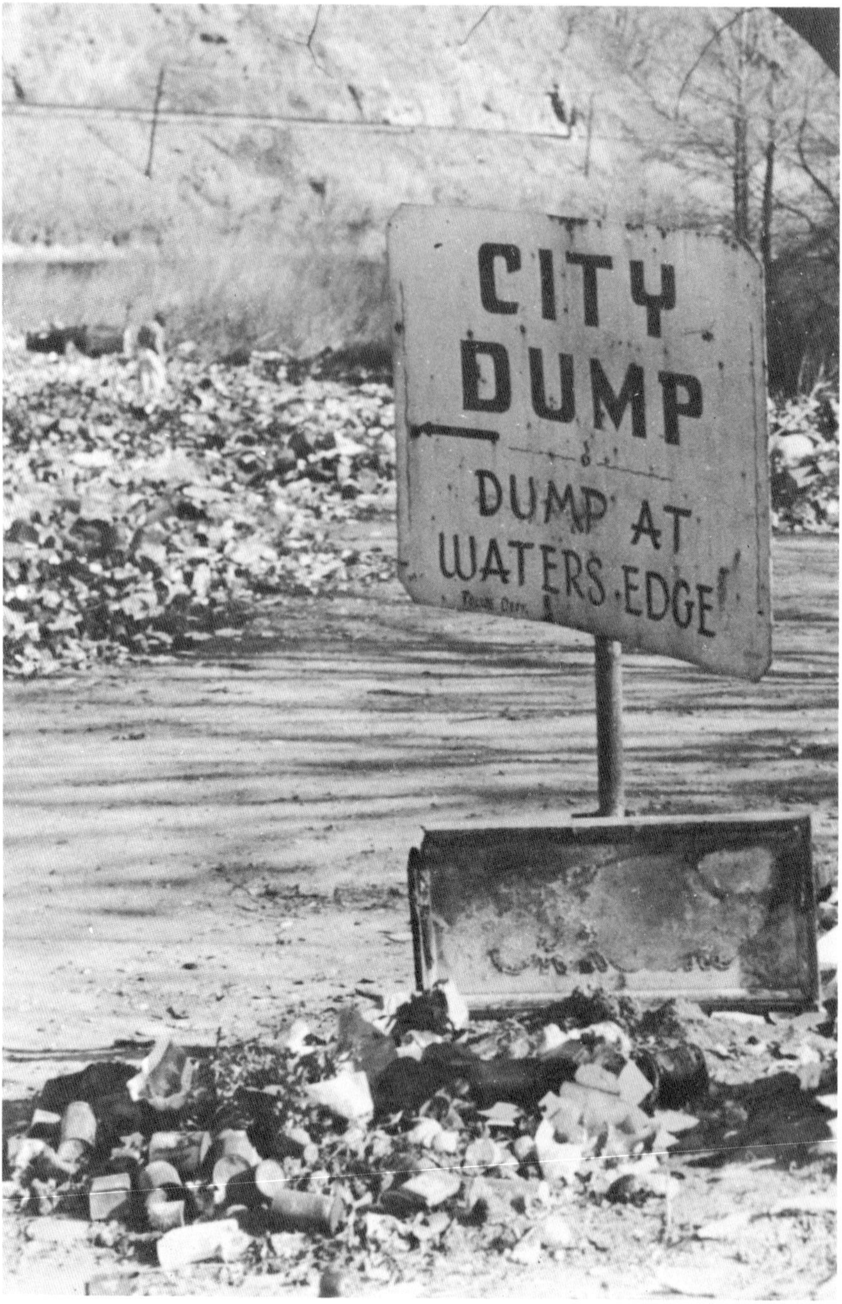
CITY
DUMP
DUMP AT
WATERS EDGE

1

Water is Man's Blood Brother

For millions of years, the oceans were the home of man's earliest ancestors—the tiny single-celled protozoa that scientists believe fathered all the living creatures of the earth. And in that simple form man's ancestors were mostly made up of water, absorbing from the sea around them all the materials they needed for survival. Now, after many millions of years of evolution, the complex animal that is man is still made up of about 70 percent water. Our bodies still must have water to function.

The blood that runs through our veins is chemically similar to salty water. Yet, inconveniently, we are not able to survive by drinking the salt water of the oceans. We need water from which much of the salt and minerals has been removed. And we need it often. No one can survive more than three or four days without providing his body with water. It does not have to be literally in the form of recognizable water; it can come from foods that contain a good percentage of water or from liquid drinks such as milk or soda pop, which are largely made up of water. But in whatever form it comes, everyone must have about two and one-half quarts of water each day.

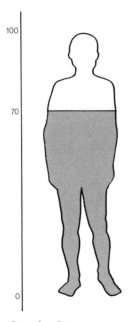

Every living thing consists mostly of water. The human body is about 70 percent water; the kangaroo rat (which lives in the desert) is 65 percent water; apples and earthworms are 80 percent; tomatoes and jellyfish, 95 percent.

Our bodies use water to operate a kind of purification plant. Water helps us to extract nourishment from food and to wash away the poisons and wastes that are produced inside the body. Within a few hours after clean water enters the body, it is excreted in the form of bodily waste, polluted by the chemicals and poisons we have to get rid of in order to remain healthy. If the water we take in is itself polluted by some form of bacteria or virus, the purification plant in the body may not be able to cope with it. Illness or even death can result.

Fresh water is just as essential to all other animals, to help their bodies operate similar purification systems. Water is also important to plants. A tree, for example, needs a combination of water, air, and sunlight for the process of *photosynthesis*. In this process, a plant combines energy from light with water and carbon dioxide to make food. An important by-product is oxygen, which is expelled into the air. Photosynthesis not only makes the tree grow, but it also is a vital link in the chain of life on which all living things depend. Man and other animals can survive only if there is plenty of oxygen in the air they breathe. They inhale oxygen and then exhale carbon dioxide, a waste product of their metabolic functions. This process completes the cycle by supplying plants with their life-giving element. The photosynthesis of plants in the ocean alone is thought to supply about 60 percent of the world's supply of oxygen.

The whole web of life on earth is filled with these kinds of delicately balanced relationships. The more men have learned about them through the years, the more they have come to respect them. Today people are beginning to realize that the old pioneering idea—that men must conquer and control nature—is arrogant and also dangerous. In spite of all his sophisticated technology, man is still a part of nature, dependent on its natural life cycles. If we can relearn a respect for the balances of nature, we will better understand the dangers of upsetting them. We will hesitate to kill even the smallest of natural organisms by polluting the waters of the earth.

The planet Earth is the only body in the solar system known to have any substantial amount of water. It is also the only one known to support any recognizable form of life. All the water on earth, in its many different forms, was released from the earth's crust as it cooled. Occasionally the earth receives a minute addition to its water supply from steam released by volcanic eruptions, but for all practical purposes the earth's water supply is now a fixed amount.

Although the earth's water supply will never be any larger, it is by no means small. After all, oceans cover 71 percent of the earth's surface. But since the oceans contain water that man and animals cannot drink, the problem is having enough usable water to sustain life.

Fortunately for mankind, the earth has its own natural system for purifying the water from the sea to the point where it is drinkable. This process is part of what is called the *hydrological cycle*. All surface water, whether in a river, lake, or ocean, continually loses part of its volume by evaporation into the air. As water evaporates, almost all of the minerals, chemicals, and pollutants that it carries are left behind. Water vapor resulting from evaporation makes clouds, which when subjected to changes in temperature release their moisture as rain and snow. This precipitation is pure, drinkable water. Much of it is dropped directly back into lakes and oceans. A tiny fraction evaporates immediately and returns to the air. Most of what falls on land runs off the surface into streams, rivers, and lakes, which eventually flow into the ocean. The rest seeps into the earth. At some stage on its way down through the ground, it lies, clean and pure, in underground reservoirs. Eventually the water reaches underground streams and rivers which also make their

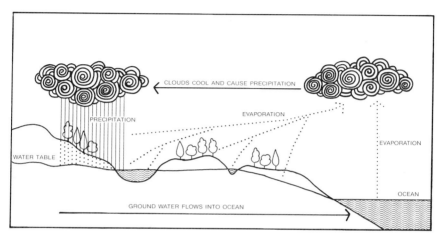

THE HYDROLOGICAL CYCLE

Water constantly evaporates from the surface of the earth and from rivers, lakes, and oceans. The water vapor rises to form clouds, leaving impurities behind. When the clouds cool, they release their moisture as rain or snow. Some of the water evaporates immediately; some runs into rivers and lakes; and some seeps through the ground and eventually rejoins the ocean. This circle of evaporation and precipitation recirculates the waters of the earth, providing clean water for all living things.

way to the ocean. Thus the hydrological cycle is repeated continuously, and the water is constantly being recirculated and reused.

Left to itself, the hydrological cycle would probably supply the earth with enough pure water for all the interrelated forms of life. But it is not being left to itself. As the world's population grows, and as technology becomes more complicated, man is increasingly polluting the water supply with all kinds of wastes and poisons. Thus it is less and less likely that there will always be a supply

Rock Creek, which flows from Maryland through Washington, D.C. Even the water in the nation's capital has not escaped damage from pollution.

of water that is fit to drink and capable of supporting every kind of life on earth. Even now it is difficult to find surface rivers and lakes of clean water. And because water picks up pollutants from the soil on its way through the earth's crust, the underground reservoirs are also becoming contaminated.

2

The Insults to Our Waters

Water pollution is not new. The waters of the earth have been defiled in one way or another since life began. Rotting vegetation has clogged up lakes and streams. Dead bodies of fish, birds, animals, and human beings have fallen or been thrown into waterways all over the world. Primitive communities have been using as their toilet the same river that supplies their water for drinking and washing—and that also supplies the water for the next community down river.

This is all natural, organic pollution. In early times, if the amount of pollution became too great and caused odor, decay, and disease, a community would usually move away and establish a new home. Gradually the water left behind was able to cleanse itself through the action of waste-consuming bacteria until it again became fresh and clean.

The consumption of waste by bacteria forms part of a natural *food chain*. The bacteria break down organic matter into its basic chemical parts, such as nitrogen compounds and hydrogen. The nitrogen compounds are food for the algae and other green underwater plants. The algae are eaten by microorganisms called *plankton*, which are eaten by fish. The fish are in turn eaten by birds, animals, and men. There are many such food chains in the many environments of the world. The chain in any particular body of water is known as its *biota*. All the organisms in a biota are interrelated; each is essential to the development of the other. If anything happens to wipe out any one link in the chain, the whole system can break down.

As the population of the world grew, and as communities gave up their nomadic habits, water came under assault from sewage, waste, and garbage to such an extent that there was just too much material for the natural waste-consuming bacteria to digest. So the water in heavily populated areas became polluted and remained polluted.

Nineteenth-century Americans were aware of the problem and realized that they would have to take action to protect their water. Brooklyn, New York, built its first sewer system in 1857. The first sewage treatment plant was built in Memphis, Tennessee, in 1880. By 1885 some states were sufficiently worried about their water to start testing it and to set up standards of purity for their water supplies. But the growth of industry and technology outstripped whatever efforts were made. Small communities grew into huge industrial cities, pouring into nearby waterways not only the wastes of the millions of people living and working there, but also the wastes of the industrial processes that made the cities prosperous. Water pollution became a permanent, accepted by-product of the modern way of life. Today, pollution comes from several sources: human sewage, agricultural chemicals, and industrial and radioactive waste.

Getting Away from It All

When two or three people are out in the wilderness, pollution from sewage is rarely a problem. The water is able to defend itself against their wastes—just as the waters of the world were able to defend themselves years ago when life was simpler and people were fewer. Campers and sportsmen are not likely to do any lasting damage to the water unless they are extraordinarily irresponsible. However, they need to understand to what extent the environment can take care of their wastes, and to what extent they could harm the places they love.

Their organic wastes, such as leftover food and body excretions, are *biodegradable*—capable of being consumed naturally by bacteria. Such wastes can safely be buried in the ground, where they will be pounced on by millions of microscopic bacteria which use them for food. The bacteria break down and purify all this natural matter to the point where it becomes part of the soil itself. The longer the wastes stay in the soil, the more complete the purification will be. So in the wilderness it is always wise to bury waste where it cannot drain too quickly into any nearby river or lake. However, small amounts of organic waste that do go directly into the water will also get a natural purification treatment. The bacteria living in the water will attack natural wastes in the same way as those on dry land do.

These natural purification systems will operate efficiently when there are just a few people doing the polluting and when the temperature is warm enough for this kind of food chain to live. (In areas of permanent frost, like parts of Alaska, very few bacteria operate; wastes buried in the ground remain there almost indefinitely without being broken down.)

Some wastes that people leave behind in wilderness areas are not consumed by the natural purification system. Even in temperate areas there are many man-made objects that bacteria have no stomach for. They don't do a bad job on paper, given enough years to work on it. After all, it is largely made of wood pulp, which is natural organic matter. But bacteria are just not interested in glass, aluminum, plastics, and similar substances. Because bacteria do not digest them and they do not, therefore, enter into any biological food chain, these materials are called *nonbiodegradables*. The combined actions of sun, wind, rain, soil, and bacteria break down biodegradables into their basic components and disperse them through the soil, streams, rivers, and lakes. But nonbiodegradables remain intact for thousands of years. Thus those who wish to preserve the beauty of the wilderness leave only biodegradable substances behind and make sure they are buried in the ground.

When a small number of people are living in an out-of-the-way place, they too may not do any lasting damage to the surrounding waterways. But because there are several people, and because they are staying in one place, they must make greater efforts not to cause pollution. Vaca-

Metal, glass, and plastic are nonbiodegradable; that is, they cannot be decomposed by natural, organic processes.

tioning in a cabin by a lake, for example, can be idyllic. There may be no one else for miles around, just wild birds and animals in the woods and fish in the lake—the lake that also provides sparkling fresh water for drinking and washing. However, unless the vacationers are careful, that water may not be as clean as it looks.

Remote cabins usually have outdoor toilets placed over a pit dug directly into the ground. This allows the wastes to seep down through the soil, being broken down by bacteria as they go. But if the pit is placed where the land slopes down to the lake, some of the waste may drain too quickly and enter the water supply before the bacteria have completed their job of purification. Again, the danger lies in numbers. When too many people use the toilet, they make so much waste that the bacteria in the soil cannot cope with it. The lake will slowly be polluted with untreated sewage.

The problem is similar on the ocean. A small yacht sailing alone at sea can pump its toilet and food wastes directly into the water without doing much damage. There are enough organisms in the vast ocean to break down the wastes and absorb them into the natural food chain. But close in to land, perhaps in a busy marina, the combined wastes of many boats will overwhelm the natural cleansing action, so that much of the waste lies in the water untreated. This condition is not only ugly and smelly, but it is also dangerous to health. People who swim at beaches nearby run the risk of infection. Also, fish in the area, which may later be caught and eaten, are feeding on untreated human excrement. Similarly, in lakes and other confined or slow-moving waters too much waste causes the natural food chain to break down, so that the water becomes putrid and unhealthy.

Thus even when a small ocean boat is within a few miles of land, its wastes should be stored in tanks and then emptied at the dockside into the local sewage treatment system. Many states now have a law requiring this to be done, but most of them do not yet enforce the law. Because of the investment necessary for building drainage lines into the sewers or for hiring trucks to haul the waste away to sewers, the law is often flouted. Many marinas just pump the untreated waste directly back into the sea, with total contempt for the environment which brings them their livelihood.

There are several other kinds of pollution that can result when people take their sport and recreation out of doors. How many sportsmen who go duck hunting realize that shotgun pellets which miss their mark and fall into the water are a threat to the ducks which make their sport? The lead pellets can poison the water and damage the ducks' food supply. Much of the exhaust from motor boats comes out under the water. It is high in carbon monoxide and therefore poisonous to fish. Gas and oil

"Poptops" are another hazard to wildlife. This fish swam inside one when quite young. As the fish matured, it was forced to grow around the metal ring.

slicks left by outboard motors are also hazardous to wildlife. They are organic and will eventually be broken down by bacteria, but it is a slow job. And in the meantime the slicks prevent sunlight from reaching plants in the water, which keeps them from completing the process of photosynthesis. This process is necessary to their existence and therefore to the existence of the entire food chain in the water.

Beautiful Neighborhoods

When people live close together, the problems of pollution from sewage multiply. Wastes cannot be simply placed in the ground or dumped in the water. Like a marina, a settled area generates too much waste for the natural processes to consume. In small rural communities, where people are scattered fairly widely over the land, domestic waste can be taken care of by a properly built septic tank for each home. All wastes are piped into a tank in the ground, where the solids drop to the bottom and eventually get decomposed by bacteria. The liquids flow out into the soil, draining under the ground or into surface rivers and lakes. As the liquids travel, they are further cleaned by the action of bacteria.

A septic tank is a fairly primitive sewage disposal system, acceptable in rural areas only if three conditions are met: First, the tank must be built where the outflow cannot seep into wells that are used for drinking water; second, the tank must be used by few enough people to avoid overloading the bacteria working on decomposition; third, the owners of the tank must be sufficiently knowledgeable and responsible to make sure that the waste contains no chemicals that are nonbiodegradable.

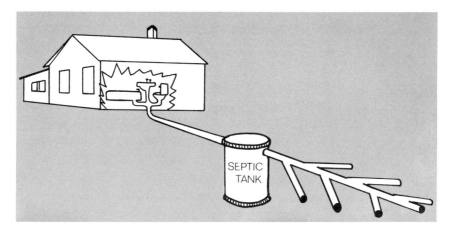

A septic tank. Solid matter settles to the bottom of the tank, and liquids flow out into the soil. Gradually all of the outflow from the house is broken down by bacteria.

But sewage tanks cost money to build, and all over the country rivers and lakes are being fouled by flows of untreated sewage from homes whose owners are unable or unwilling to install septic tanks.

In towns and suburbs, wastes must be drained into sewer systems instead of septic tanks. People live much too close together to be able to use the natural cleansing action of bacteria in the soil and water for their household wastes. Also, life in these larger communities tends to become more complicated than it is in rural areas; sewage is generated in much greater quantities and consists of many different kinds of waste. Each of millions of suburban homes has several toilets, two or three bathtubs and showers, a washing machine, a dishwasher, and an automatic garbage disposal—all of which work by taking in clean water, loading it with impurities, and then flushing it away. Donald Carr, in his book *Death of Sweet Waters*, gives the following statistics on water use: Poor people in a tropical country use less than 5 gallons of water a day per person. A rural community in England uses about 20 gallons per person each day. In large English towns each person uses about 50 gallons per day, and in similar large towns in the United States the figure is close to 200 gallons per person each day. The residents of Beverly Hills, California, use the largest amount of water per person in the world—500 gallons each day.

Towns and suburbs load up all this water with more than just ordinary human waste. Many washing machines and dishwashers work efficiently only with detergents—the "wonder" cleaning agents that get everything "cleaner than clean." However, in the quantities in which they are now being used, detergents may be doing permanent damage to the nation's freshwater lakes. By law, all detergents must be biodegradable, so that they can be broken down by bacteria. However, septic tanks and most sewage treatment plants are unable to remove the *phosphates* in detergents. These chemicals, scientists believe, act as nutrients to algae in lakes, causing them to become overactive and grow too fast. When the algae die, their decomposition uses up the oxygen out of the water. This is because in the process of decay chemicals oxidize, or combine with the free oxygen dissolved in the water. Soon there is not enough oxygen in the water for the plankton and the fish to breathe. Consequently, the whole natural food chain of the lake breaks down. The natural aging of the lake, called *eutrophication*, has been greatly accelerated—by tens of thousands of years. The lake ends up dead, useless to man and beast. In some areas as much as one-half of the phosphate which is believed to cause

Phosphates from detergents nourish algae and other underwater plants, eventually causing the lake to become a swamp. Lake Picaro, Minnesota, has suffered additional abuse as well, evidenced by the discarded automobile.

accelerated eutrophication comes from detergents. (Some, too, comes from fertilizers that are washed into lakes from farmyards and lawns.)

Detergent manufacturers are struggling now with the problem of finding an efficient substitute for phosphates, one that will cause no damage to the nation's water. A few brands of phosphate-free detergents are on the market, and concerned citizens are buying them, even though their cost is usually high. Other people are resolving to use smaller amounts of detergent and to buy the brands that are lower in phosphate than others. Also, of course, everyone can run washing machines and automatic dishwashers less frequently.

But few people whose homes are connected to sewer systems even stop to think where all the liquid *effluent* goes when they use washing machines, flush toilets, or drain sinks and bathtubs. They take it for granted that once anything goes down the sewer someone else is taking care of its treatment and disposal. But is this always true? The following examples help answer this question.

In Miami, Florida, students conducted a simple experiment: they put dye and peanut hulls into toilets in shoreline hotels. When the dye and peanut hulls appeared

Heavy algae growth in a freshwater lake

unchanged in Biscayne Bay, it became obvious that the hotels were discharging untreated sewage directly into the ocean.

Off the coast of California, sea urchins have flourished in such extravagant numbers that they have stripped away many of the underwater kelp forests. What has nourished the sea urchins is the outfall of sewage from Los Angeles. (No one knows what effects the death of the kelp beds will have on the natural food chains on the Pacific coast.)

In fact, in the mid-1960s almost 20 million people were still discharging raw sewage into the nation's waterways. Mitchell Gordon, in his book *Sick Cities*, says that one-fourth of all the waste which cities are sending into streams is raw, untreated sewage. Another one-third has had only slight treatment, either because efficient sewage treatment plants have not been built or because they are overloaded.

The reasons for these shocking statistics are many. First, the treatment of sewage is a complicated, expensive process requiring specialized knowledge and equipment. Sewage is over 99 percent liquid. The first, or primary, stage of its treatment is to strain out all the large solids. Then the water is passed through a series of tanks in which remaining solids (called sludge) can settle to the bottom. Later the sludge is taken out and either burned or used for fertilizer. The secondary stage of treatment removes harmful organisms and fine particles. The water may be filtered through a bed of sand and rocks, where it is cleaned by the action of bacteria. Or sometimes the water is aerated at this stage; that is, oxygen is added to act on some of the impurities. Finally, the water stands in

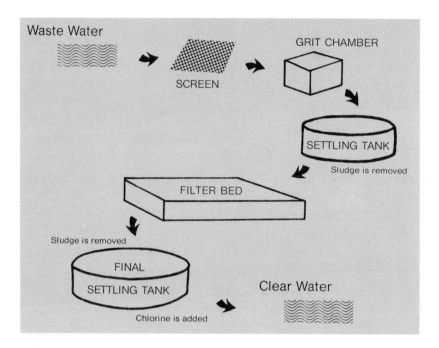

Waste Water

SCREEN

GRIT CHAMBER

SETTLING TANK

Sludge is removed

FILTER BED

Sludge is removed

FINAL

SETTLING TANK

Clear Water

Chlorine is added

The treatment of sewage. In the primary stage, the large solids are removed. The fine particles and harmful bacteria are taken out in the secondary stage. Radioactive waste, phosphates, and other chemicals are still present, however, unless the effluent is given a third treatment.

another tank, where the last sludge settles out. Then the effluent is chlorinated before being run off into a river, lake, or ocean. Chlorine sterilizes the water by killing disease-carrying bacteria. These methods of treatment— which may vary a little from one plant to another—take care of organic wastes satisfactorily. However, they do not remove chemicals like the phosphates from detergents. This can only be done by a third, or tertiary, process, an expensive chemical cleaning, which only a few cities operate at present.

As small communities have grown into cities, their sewage treatment and disposal plants have not always kept pace with the increase in population. Treatment to a high enough standard to avoid all pollution of natural waterways is a complex and technical business that communities are not always willing to finance.

Some cities that do have efficient treatment plants do not always process all their sewage. This is another reason that so much untreated waste pours into this country's water supplies. Sometimes the community has not voted enough money for the plant to operate 24 hours a day, so that the plant is regularly shut down for a few hours. Sometimes the staff does not operate the plant properly. At least one state, Iowa, is making an effort to meet this problem; it has set up training programs for workers in sewage treatment plants and is requiring them to pass examinations before they can be promoted to supervisory positions. In many states, however, operating the treatment plants is a job left to untrained personnel.

One of the biggest problems preventing sewage plants from treating all the water is overloading. In many cities storm drains run into the sewers, so that a heavy rainstorm results in a tremendous increase in the amount of water to be processed. Almost all the nation's treatment plants are unable to cope with these peak loads. Thus after a storm the water must bypass the plants. All the effluent, both untreated sewage and storm water, goes directly into the waterways.

Every time untreated sewage gets into the water supply, it increases the problem of getting water that is clean enough to drink. People have always taken their drinking water from freshwater streams, rivers, and lakes, and from wells that tap underground reservoirs. But more and more of these supplies are being polluted.

The waters of Lake Michigan in Montrose Harbor, Chicago. Before Chicago residents can drink water from Lake Michigan, it must undergo an expensive and complicated purification process.

The Hudson River, for example, is so polluted that much of it can no longer be relied upon to provide water for the cities along its banks. Chicago's drinking water comes from Lake Michigan, but it may not do so much longer because of all the sewage and industrial waste that is discharged into the lake.

The warning has been clear for years. And some communities are beginning to listen. The Whittier Narrows water reclamation plant, in the Los Angeles area, treats millions of gallons of sewage a day. The solid matter is settled out, and then the remainder is treated with bacteria and with chlorine, in the usual way. But after that, the water is given a nearly unique purifying treatment. It is pumped into spreading basins from which, over a period of time, it trickles down through the soil to join the underground waters. It is then pumped up again from wells and goes into circulation as fresh, pure water.

High in the Sierra Nevada in northern California is beautiful Lake Tahoe, whose water is a brilliant clear turquoise blue. As the community along the lake's southern shore grew, the residents decided to stop discharging sewage into the lake. They realized that their effluents would soon destroy the lake's beauty and the quality of its water by stimulating the growth of algae. So they embarked on an eight-year program to build what many people consider to be the most advanced waste treatment system in the world. All sewage from the community goes to a very sophisticated treatment plant which adds extra filtering and chemical treatment to the normal primary and secondary treatment. Then the effluent, by now well cleaned, is pumped through a 27-mile-long pipe, up 1,235 feet over a mountain, into a new man-made lake. The water is stored there, to be used during the summer for irrigation. Rainbow trout have been introduced to the new lake and are thriving. In addition, plans are being made to use the lake for water sports.

Over half of the money for building this system came from Lake Tahoe residents. Some came from federal grants; some from a loan by the state of California; and some from the United States Forest Service. The cost was high—about $28 million—but Lake Tahoe is protected, and the people who spent the money will make sure that no one else defiles the lake in which they invested so much.

Unfortunately, the examples of successful battles against water pollution from domestic wastes are all too few. And each day the problems become more serious. The United States uses about 350 billion gallons of water a day, and the figure is rising steadily. In 10 years' time, the country will probably use 600 billion gallons a day. In another 20 years, it may use almost 1,000 billion gallons a day. To help meet this kind of demand, the nation must begin to clean the water as it is used and return it into circulation as pure as it was originally. The best and ultimately the cheapest way to increase the supply of usable water is to eliminate pollution.

In the 1960s United States cities spent $3 billion building new sewage treatment plants and updating old ones. However, the Department of the Interior has estimated that the government needs to spend $15 billion to help clean up the country's rivers and lakes. (This is about the amount the United States spent in six months on the Indochina war.) The money would be invested mostly in subsidizing sewage treatment. In addition, it would be used to set up control facilities to prevent pollution from municipalities and industrial plants. Many knowledgeable engineers think that this will not be enough money. When they include the cost of cleaning up industrial pollution too, their figures go as high as $20 billion a year for 10 years—or $10 per person per year. This seems to be a small price to pay for preserving the water that supports all life on earth.

The Good Earth

When city dwellers feel harassed by pollution and overcrowding, they get romantic ideas about life on the farm. "That's where the good life is," they tell themselves. "Out there with fresh air and pure water, where man lives close to the earth and treats it with respect." Unfortunately, the truth is disappointing; the dream of rural purity has become an illusion.

Life on the farm has turned into Big Business, and it is one of the major sources of water pollution. Large corporations, striving always for larger profits, are quick to take advantage of technological aids that help produce bigger yields. These technological aids are primarily chemicals. Seeds are dipped in chemical fungicides to protect them from rot. Weeds are destroyed by chemical herbicides. The land is enriched by organic and chemical fertilizers. These chemicals may at first help to produce more food, but they are spreading death and destruction to all living creatures, including man—not just on the farmers' own lands but throughout the world.

When rain falls on soil or foliage treated with these chemicals, it carries them along as it runs off into streams and lakes. Insects and microscopic life take in the chemicals while feeding on vegetation in the water. In turn, they pass the chemicals along the food chain; they are eaten by slightly larger animals, who are eaten by larger animals, and so forth. At each step of the chain, *biological amplification* occurs. This means that the amount of the chemical becomes more concentrated in each creature as it moves up the chain. A microorganism, for example, may contain one part of chemical for every million parts of itself. A bug eats many microorganisms, and perhaps he has in his body 18 parts of chemical per million. In a larger bug, the dose may go up to 1,000 parts per million. Then fish that eat the larger bugs can accumulate perhaps 30,000 parts per million. Thus a man who eats such fish will take in large doses of poison. Some filter-feeding animals, like oysters and clams, concentrate the chemicals to a far higher degree than others. When they eat, they take in large amounts of water, strain out the small organisms, and pass the water out of their systems. In this manner they can absorb great quantities of contaminated micro-organisms.

Many of the chemicals that have been used in agriculture are dangerously poisonous. DDT, for example, damages growth of plankton and plants in the water. As little

A baby eagle rests next to an egg that never hatched, probably because its shell was too thin. An accumulation of DDT in the mother eagle's body could have been the cause.

as 0.00006 parts per million can destroy an entire shrimp population. And DDT can cause birds to lay eggs with shells too thin for the embryo chicks to survive. Robins can die from eating earthworms contaminated with DDT.

Another pesticide, endrin, was responsible for the death of huge quantities of fish in the Mississippi River. In the fall of 1960 the lower Mississippi, from Memphis to the Gulf of Mexico, at times became a river of mysterious and large-scale death. Schools of fish disturbed by the propellers of tugboats darted to the surface, where they went into convulsions and died. In the fall and winter of 1963, approximately 5 million fish died in this way. A government investigation found low levels of several pesticides in samples of river water, and high concentrations in the bodies of the dead fish. Finally endrin pesticide, which is used to protect cotton and sugar cane from insects, was tracked down as the killer. Endrin is a chlorinated hydrocarbon—a powerful and long-lasting nerve poison.

Endosulfan, another pesticide, caused widespread destruction of fish in Germany's River Rhine. Seventeen people died in Mexico after the pesticide parathion got into the bread supply. Many farm workers have died and others have been disabled by the same pesticide. Three members of a family in New Mexico were grotesquely disabled after eating meat from pigs which had been fed on grain treated with a mercury fungicide. Studies by the National Cancer Institute suggest that 50 out of 130 widely used pesticides are capable of causing serious illnesses, including leukemia. There are indications also that some of them cause genetic damage by altering the DNA molecule.

33

This discarded pesticide barrel was used, with several others, to float a boat dock in Lake Wappapello, Missouri. The barrels were removed by Missouri conservation officials after several thousand fish were found dead.

The increased use of chemicals in farming has several other effects. High potency fertilizers get washed off into rivers and streams, where their phosphates cause accelerated eutrophication, just as phosphates from detergents do. Some spray herbicides and weed killers are nutrients; others are toxic poisons.

One of the most complicated problems caused by the chemicals is a change in the balance of nature. In Malaysia, for example, DDT was sprayed on crops to kill a disease that was stunting their growth. The DDT was eaten by insects, which were eaten by larger bugs, which were then eaten by rats. By the time the rats were eaten by cats, the DDT had concentrated into large enough amounts to kill the cats. The cats died and were no longer able to control the rats. So the rats multiplied out of control, ran wild, and attacked human beings, infecting them with diseases.

In the face of these consequences, why do farmers—and enthusiastic gardeners—use chemicals? It is a simple question to which there are only complicated answers.

One important justification for pesticides is that they have saved countless numbers of lives by controlling malaria, cholera, typhus, and other killer diseases spread by insects. And fungicides, herbicides, and fertilizers, as well as pesticides, have made it possible to grow food where none would grow before—to feed people who were starving. These products have also enabled farmers below the poverty level to grow good crops and prosper, so that they and their families could have a decent living. In addition, when the chemicals were first marketed, no one knew what damage they would do.

As the dangers continue to be discovered, action is being taken. But it is a slow process. A farmer who has seen nothing more than a few dead robins is not easily convinced that the chemicals he is using have a cumulative effect all around the world. Manufacturers are not easily convinced that a product in which they have invested millions of dollars is doing more harm than good. As a result, legislation seems to be the only hope.

Governments everywhere have passed laws against the use of the more dangerous chemical products. In many nations, the use of DDT has been banned. Early in 1970 the Olin Corporation, which made about 20 percent of the DDT produced in the United States, ceased production completely. Two years later, the agricultural use of DDT was virtually banned in the United States. The pesticide may still be used in epidemic emergencies, however.

The government has also taken action against the use of products containing 2,4,5-T. This is a chemical that was developed and tested for biological warfare. It was used widely as a weed killer and also as a defoliant in Vietnam, where it was sprayed on more than half a million acres. The 2,4,5-T passed from the land into drinking water supplies and so into human beings, and persistent reports came from Vietnam of birth defects and miscarriages in villages contaminated by 2,4,5-T. Laboratory tests on mice confirmed that there are genetic dangers from this chemical. The use of 2,4,5-T was restricted.

Even though these chemicals are no longer in general use, their effects will be slow to pass out of the world's life cycles. Five years after Connecticut had stopped spraying its woodlands with DDT, fish in the rivers and lakes were showing only a 20 percent decrease in contamination. The *half-life* of DDT is about 18 years. That is, a concentration of DDT in body tissue now will be reduced to half its strength in 18 years, to half again in another 18 years, and so on.

In 1970 the United States Public Health Service carried out a series of tests on the water supplies of various communities throughout the country. They found that nearly all the samples showed traces of pesticides and that many samples also showed excessive amounts of other chemicals.

Beside such sinister chemical poisoning, the old earthy problem of animal sewage may not seem very alarming. Yet that too is one of the facts of agricultural pollution. Nearly 1.3 billion tons of agricultural manure and waste are produced in the United States each year. Most of this refuse is carried by rain water directly off pasture lands into streams, rivers, and lakes. Animal excretions cause death and decay in the waters of the earth in the same way that the untreated wastes from cities do.

Building for the Future

Real estate development and road building seem to be an inevitable part of American life. To house the estimated growth in population by the year 2000, the United States will need to build each week the houses, factories, and roads equivalent to a city for 100,000 people. It is important to understand what this will do to the waters of the nation. Highway and building construction is only one of the many industries in the United States, and like the others, it makes its own unique contribution to water pollution.

When rain falls on land covered with natural vegetation, it seeps into the soil, nourishing the plants that grow there and thus nurturing the entire food chain that depends upon them. The water slowly drains into the ground and joins the water table, becoming a source of water for man to tap. But the building of homes and roads can prevent this from happening. To clear the necessary acres of land, construction companies usually bring in huge earth-moving machines that level the entire area and remove the vegetation. When the natural growth has been stripped away, rain runs off the surface of the land instead of penetrating the soil. As the water travels, it carries away the topsoil, creates gulleys and washes, and becomes polluted before man has an opportunity to use it. When land is covered with concrete paving, this too prevents the

When builders strip away natural vegetation, erosion is the inevitable result, as shown in this photograph of a development in Louisiana. Erosion, in turn, causes siltation of nearby rivers and lakes.

rain from seeping into the soil. The water runs off the
surface into drains and sewers, carrying whatever dirt and
pollution it has picked up on its way. It then becomes part
of the sewage water without ever being a source of fresh
water.

Removal of the natural vegetation during construction
also causes *siltation* of freshwater lakes and streams.
When a new development is near a waterway, rain washes
large amounts of the topsoil into the water, making it
dark and murky. The silt can kill the plants in the water
by cutting off the sunlight they need for photosynthesis.
When these plants die, they no longer provide oxygen for
other organisms in the water. And when the oxygen count
drops, these and other organisms die and use up still more

oxygen when they decompose. When the entire biota—
bacteria, plankton, and fish—dies, the water putrefies.

In both real estate development and highway construction silting is usually temporary. It stops when the project
is finished and there is no loose soil left to wash away.
However, the effects of the silting may not go away so
quickly. Slow running streams and lakes can grope their
way back to life only through a gradual process that may
take as long as 15 or 20 years.

Building and highway development is also damaging
the nation's great salt marshes. Over 2 million acres have
already been dredged, drained, or filled—more than one-

Siltation is especially noticeable in reservoirs. As the water stands,
the mud and sand settle on the bottom and gradually fill up the lake.
This Virginia reservoir, which has been drained, accumulated great
quantities of dirt from eroded areas nearby.

fourth of the total. Land-hungry men see the marshes as useless, not realizing that when the marshes are destroyed an entire chain of life dies. Birds, animals, fish, and shellfish disappear, and soon the sea and the wind smell like rotten eggs. The salt marshes that are as yet untouched by man are teeming with rich plant and animal life. In these marshes, hundreds of small animals and birds—a combination of those who belong to the land and those who belong to the sea—find the nesting places and cover in cold weather that are essential to wildlife. Animals, fish, insects, bacteria—all live in a delicately balanced harmony. The life systems of the salt marshes are as much a part of the world as man is, and it is becoming increasingly clear that a desire for profitable real estate is not sufficient reason to wipe them out.

The increasing amount of urban development has yet another consequence. The tons of concrete being used are made from two-thirds water mixed with one-third solids. Some of this water evaporates into the atmosphere as the concrete dries, but a little water is permanently locked up, withdrawn from circulation in the hydrological cycle. Continued development is reducing the amount of water that is present on the earth to support life.

Power for the People

One November evening in 1965 an electric power failure blacked out New York and other cities in the northeastern United States for several hours. This brought home to Americans, as nothing had done before, how much their metropolitan life styles depend on electric power. The darkness that night was frightening and dangerous. People were trapped in elevators and in the subways.

There was no electric heat. Pumps for water supplies and sewage treatment systems failed. Movie and television screens went blank. Actors were left floundering on Broadway's stages while their audiences were trapped in their seats by the darkness. Hospitals had to switch to emergency generators to keep life-saving heart machines and kidney machines functioning.

The demand for electricity increases every year. In 1959 a typical American family used about 3,650 kilowatt-hours of electric power. (One kilowatt is 1,000 watts, the amount of electricity used by a 100-watt bulb turned on for 10 hours.) By 1969 a similar family was using 6,550 kilowatt-hours. In the same 10 years the amount of electricity used by commerce and industry doubled. The total use during 1968 in the United States averaged out to 7,167 kilowatt-hours per person, compared with 3,563 in Great Britain and 2,877 in West Germany. Estimates for the future are that the use of electricity in the United States will double every 10 years.

But can the country afford this increase? Electricity may be penny cheap, as power companies advertise, but no one knows the price of the damage caused to the nation's water by the production of electric power. In all three processes used to generate electric power—hydroelectric plants, fossil fuel plants, and atomic power plants—water is a vital ingredient, and pollution is possible.

A hydroelectric power plant uses the energy of water falling over a dam to drive turbines, which create electricity. This is a clean process; that is, it dumps no pollutants into the water or the air. However, it has a profound effect on the river. Above the dam a big reservoir forms, backing up into the tributary rivers and streams for perhaps hundreds of miles. The free flow of all these waterways is affected, with a chain reaction on their plant and animal life. Fast running streams which are changed into sluggish backwaters can no longer support the same wildlife as before. Some creatures die out, and when this happens the chain of life in the water is damaged or destroyed.

Fossil fuel plants are so called because they run their turbines by burning fuels that come out of the ground — oil, coal, and natural gas. These plants pollute the water supply in two ways. As the fuel burns, it gives off fumes containing ash and chemicals. These pollutants eventually settle on the ground and are washed by rainfall into rivers and lakes.

Fossil fuel power plants also pump billions of gallons of water out of a river and use it to cool the operating equipment. When the water is returned to the river a short distance downstream, it is approximately 10 to 25 degrees warmer than when it was pumped out. The addition of heat to a body of water is called *thermal pollution*, and it has disturbing effects on the natural life of the river. Thermal pollution causes the algae in the water to grow too fast. It also stimulates poisonous blue green algae to bloom. This affects the plankton and indirectly the fish, so that the whole biota of the river is damaged. The warmth has a direct effect on fish as well, causing disease and death. They die by the million, possibly as many as 200 million each year. The heat also acts upon wastes and chemicals already discharged into the river farther upstream, often converting them into toxic poisons.

Atomic power plants are the newest sources of electric

A hydroelectric power plant

A fossil fuel plant

A nuclear power plant

power. They also use tremendous quantities of water for cooling and discharge heated water back into the river. But these plants raise the water to higher temperatures than fossil fuel plants do. Thus the thermal pollution from an atomic power plant is even more harmful.

But added to this is the more sinister possibility of radioactive pollution from nuclear power plants. Tritium, one of the few substances in the world that is not purified out by evaporation in the hydrological cycle, is one potential pollutant. Once tritium enters the waterways, it accumulates in all the biological processes of nature. Its primary threat is that it may damage the DNA molecule, which is at the root of man's genetic inheritance.

In the United States, the Atomic Energy Commission is required by law to regulate the amount of pollution by radioactive waste. Many scientists believe that the commission's regulations are not strict enough, partly because the AEC has the responsibility to promote nuclear development as well as to control its dangers. Some scientists say that the AEC is wrong to declare certain amounts of radioactivity to be "safe." They point out that any amount is potentially dangerous because it accumulates in the body, and because its effects may be passed on from one generation to another. There is also well-documented evidence that radioactive pollution can cause cancer and leukemia.

The saddest thing about pollution from power plants is that most of it is unnecessary. The technology exists that makes it possible to avoid nearly all the damage the plants do to the environment. As awareness of the dangers of pollution increases, citizens and governments are growing more insistent that power companies conform to stricter regulations and recycle their water or contain their wastes.

In Vermont an atomic power plant was intending to use two-thirds of the flow of the Connecticut River and heat the water up by 20 degrees before returning it. But the state imposed limits on the thermal pollution, allowing almost no discharge of heat in the summer. So the power company had to install cooling towers at a cost of $6 million. In Florida the Justice Department filed a lawsuit against the Florida Light and Power Company to stop it from polluting the waters of Biscayne Bay. The combined efforts of Minnesota's Pollution Control Agency and a citizens' group called MECCA forced the Northern States Power Company to build extra safeguards against pollution into its new nuclear power plant on the Mississippi River.

Power companies are reluctant to spend millions of dollars for controlling pollution, recycling their cooling water, and trapping their effluents of ash, chemicals, and radioactive wastes. In the past, their job has been simply to provide electricity at the lowest possible price; only now are they beginning to see that environmental factors may be just as important as low cost, if not more so.

In a Gallup poll, three-fourths of the people questioned said that they would be prepared to pay more for their electricity in order to preserve the environment. And although the investment at the power plant runs into millions of dollars, by the time that extra cost is spread over all the users of electricity, the addition to a householder's bill will be only a few cents. The figure varies according to who is doing the arithmetic, but the cost of efficient pollution control for power companies lies somewhere between $.50 and $5 per resident per year.

The Industrial Merry-go-round

To make enough paper for one copy of this book, a manufacturer had to use approximately 100 gallons of water. In one year, the mills in the United States that produce paper products use about 2,000 billion gallons of the nation's water. And by the late 1960s they were cleaning only one-third of this amount before dumping it back into the waterways, loaded with pollutants of various kinds.

Paper is made by dissolving wood pulp, sulfur, and other chemicals in water. This mixture is then rolled over vacuum presses that take out the water and leave a film of paper to be dried, finished, and polished. By the time the water has completed its job of making paper, it has become a thick sludgy liquid infected with sulfur, mercury, and other toxic chemicals. For years this liquid was pumped out directly into rivers—downstream, of course, from the point where the mill took in its water supply— and sent on its way, making the river unusable for anyone else within miles. Bark, which is stripped from the trees that are used as pulp, was often thrown into the river also.

Very slowly, local, state, and federal laws are forcing paper manufacturers to install expensive equipment to clean up the water they use before it goes back into circulation. At some paper mills the polluted sludge is now being pumped into big basins, where the solids settle out and are removed. Some companies are taking out the sulfur and other chemicals so that they can be used again. Bark is being saved and made into profitable wallboard.

When the Kimberly Clark Corporation, for example, built a new mill in California, the company came up

Action Lake Erie

Hammermill has a new $35,000,000 stake in Erie, Pennsylvania

On December 27, 1968, Hammermill Paper Company awarded a $35-million contract for the design and construction of pollution abatement and pulp mill facilities at its Erie (Pa.) Division. The new facilities include a solution to pollution control problems the paper manufacturer has faced since it converted to mixed Pennsylvania hardwood pulping operation in the early 1950's.

No pollution abatement effort by a major, established industry is simple. Hammermill has spent more than $4-million in treatment and disposal facilities, research and development in the last nine years alone in the search for a practical answer to its problems. The present $35-million program is the result. Why was the answer so long in coming? Why has it cost so much? The complex problems faced by Hammermill and the methods and techniques used to solve them prompt meaningful questions that require straight answers.

Answer. The collected pulping liquors are injected into the deep disposal wells located on Hammermill property at the Erie Division. The bleach plant wastes are discharged into Lake Erie and currently pose the major control problem for Hammermill.

Question. Are Hammermill's wastes harmful in any way?

Answer. Absolutely not. The wastes will not cause algae growth and are not harmful to aquatic life, animals or humans.

Question. Does Hammermill pollute the swimming beaches?

Answer. Not on your life.

Question. If the wastes are not harmful, why are they objectionable to the State?

Answer. Because of their foam, color and demand for dissolved oxygen from the Lake waters. The State maintains strict treatment requirements for wastes with a dissolved oxygen demand.

Question. Do other types of wastes have this demand for dissolved oxygen?

Answer. Definitely. One of the most severe problems is the oxygen demand of raw or insufficiently-treated sewage.

Question. Is raw or insufficiently-treated sewage a problem in the Erie (Pa.) area?

Answer. Yes. The many farms, small towns and septic tanks outside our primary metropolitan area contribute a large volume of untreated runoff to the Lake. Erie's own treatment plant will be unable to cope with its increasing loads from a growing city. Under certain conditions, this can contribute to the problems of dissolved oxygen demand and algae growth.

Question. Is algae also a pollution problem?

Answer. Yes. In addition to being a general nuisance to fishermen, boating and swimming, algae also creates severe odors and oxygen demand as it rots along shorelines.

Question. What makes algae grow so fast?

Answer. The tremendous amounts of phosphates and nitrates going into the Lake each day. These materials known as nutrients come from sewage and agricultural runoff. Experts generally agree that algae and untreated sewage currently pose the biggest pollution threats to Lake Erie.

Question. Do Hammermill wastes contribute phosphates and nitrates to the Lake?

An announcement by Hammermill Paper Company of its plans to reduce pollution in Lake Erie. In recent years, paper manufacturers have taken steps to clean up the water they discharge into rivers and lakes.

against such strict controls set by the state's Water Pollution Control Board that it had to put in the cleanest paper mill ever built. In Alabama, the same company spent $2.5 million on a process to remove 98 percent of the insoluble pollution from its effluent before returning the

47

water to the Coosa River. International Paper budgeted $101 million over a four-year period to control air and water pollution at all its plants in the United States. These actions will be a vast improvement on the irresponsible manufacturing methods of earlier years. (In fact, there is no longer any reason for paper mills to cause water pollution. It is now possible to build a closed circuit system for the water, cleaning it up so that it can be recycled continuously.)

Paper mills are by no means the only industrial polluters. Hundreds and thousands of manufacturing processes depend on a regular supply of water, often in huge quantities. A Senate committee on water resources has forecast that by 1980 industry will pass through its plants 65 percent or more of all the fresh water used in the United States.

Steel manufacture is another large industry that uses a tremendous amount of water. In 1967 American metal manufacturers used 4,578 billion gallons of water—and partially cleaned up only about one-fourth of this amount. The remainder was simply discharged into rivers and lakes. It takes 70,000 to 110,000 gallons of water to make one ton of steel, mostly in cooling processes of various kinds, including dipping the metal into water. Oils, acids, and phenols (poisonous carbon compounds) run out with the waste water. Again, this water could be cleaned and recycled; it is technologically possible. But so far no company has done so. For its polluting activities, the U.S. Steel Corporation in Chicago was taken to court and fined. But it was cheaper to pay the fine than to set up the equipment needed to prevent pollution.

Meatpacking plants also are notorious polluters of our

waters. Each weekday in the United States almost 500,000 meat animals go to market for slaughter and processing. The industry supports about 175,000 workers in some 3,000 plants around the country. All of these plants use water to prepare the meat for sale in its various forms. Water is used to wash down the animals, to flush out the blood and wastes during slaughtering, and to clean the meat and the equipment. Sometimes the water carries its load of blood and wastes into the sewers, for whatever treatment the municipality provides. But all too often it runs off directly into a nearby waterway without treatment of any kind, staining the water red, covering it with fat and animal waste, and damaging or killing the natural life in the water.

The Merrimack River becomes clogged with blood and other animal wastes when it passes the Manchester, New Hampshire, slaughterhouse, which discharges its filthy water directly into the river. For years the Missouri River and its tributaries have carried foul pollution from the meatpacking plants around Omaha, Nebraska. The meatpackers of Sioux City, Iowa, dump stinking offal into the Missouri and pollute the waters of four states. In Troy, New York, the Hudson River is thick with chicken entrails. Some of these crimes have been the subject of hearings held by the Public Health Service, but the pollution still has not been halted.

The nation's giant chemical corporations also have huge quantities of refuse to get rid of. Much of it is suspended in the water that they use to manufacture products like detergents, plastics, fertilizers, and drugs. When this water is discharged directly into streams and lakes, it carries with it vast quantities of chemical wastes. Some

49

An aerial view of the Merrimack River (above). Although the river looks beautiful from this distance, it actually contains the same ugly pollutants that are pouring into the waters near Omaha, Nebraska (below). The blood from meatpacking plants stains the rivers red brown, and the grease floats in clumps on top of the water.

of the wastes are immediately poisonous to the natural life of the river; others concentrate, in the way that DDT does, all the way up the food chain until they reach a point at which they kill. Mercury is one of the most persistent of these chemical wastes. It is used in many major industries, including those that produce fungicides, paint, plastics, paper, and fertilizers. In Japan 60 people died of poisoning and more than 50 were disabled after they ate fish contaminated with mercury. The chemical had been discharged as waste into the Minamata River by a plastics manufacturer. People living as far apart as Pakistan, Iraq, Guatemala, and New Mexico have suffered dreadful illnesses from mercury poisoning, frequently with permanent brain damage. Mercury has been found in pheasants in Montana and in chickens in South Dakota.

For 15 or 20 years the Dow Chemical Company of Canada discharged mercury into the St. Clair River, which runs into Lake St. Clair, through Detroit, and into Lake Erie. At times the plant dumped 200 pounds of mercury a day. Wyandotte, another chemical company, put between 10 and 20 pounds of mercury a day into the Detroit River, which also runs into Lake Erie. In 1970, mercury in these waters reached such dangerous levels that the Canadian government and the states of Michigan and Ohio ordered a ban on all fishing in Lake St. Clair, the Detroit River, and the western end of Lake Erie. The chemical companies were ordered to cease discharging mercury at all, and lawsuits were begun to collect for the damage that had been caused.

Mercury is picked up, it is believed, by microorganisms, which pass it along the food chain. Through the process of biological amplification, the amount of mercury has been multiplied by as much as 4,000 times when it reaches the large fish. Estimated "safe" levels of mercury vary between the .05 parts per million stipulated by the World Health Organization and the .5 parts per million agreed upon by the Canadian and United States governments. When the ban on fishing was imposed, mercury levels as high as 7 parts per million had been found in walleyed pike taken from Lake St. Clair.

Some industries, like the paper industry, are beginning to spend large sums of money to tackle the problems of pollution. The Ford Motor Company, under the leadership of Henry Ford II, spent $66 million in the 1960s to reduce air and water pollution. Then the company increased this amount to $60 million for 1970 alone. DuPont, which probably makes more chemical products than anyone else, was spending $10 million on water and air pollution control in 1967 and $118 million in 1968. The company was spending over $200 million by 1973. In a 10-year period, the number of people DuPont had working on environmental control grew from 250 to 650. Many other manufacturers are showing their concern over pollution with enlarged budgets of this kind.

But the fight is not an easy one—even for industrialists who *want* to avoid pollution. In the free enterprise system of the United States, industry is constantly under pressure to meet competition by keeping prices down. If a sugar refiner, for example, spends large sums of money on recycling the wastes of his refinery so that they cause no water pollution, then his final product will cost a little more. A housewife will see this product on the shelves of her supermarket at one or two cents a pound more than sugar of identical quality which has been refined by a company that is spending no money on pollution control. All her instincts and consumer training tell her to buy the cheaper sugar. So the conscientious refiner will suffer economic hardship if he is the only one to install expensive pollution control equipment.

Also, it is often true that the benefits of pollution control go primarily to people who do not pay for them. A factory on a river, for example, may spend hundreds of thousands of dollars to clean up the water it uses. But the person who uses the water downstream, not the factory, gets the benefits from the expensive equipment.

One solution to these problems lies in federal regulations to set water quality standards that are identical all over the country and that are enforced with equal vigor. This would prevent irresponsible manufacturers from prospering at the expense of those who are taking action to protect the environment. It would also prevent companies from fighting off local pollution controls by threatening to remove their plant, and the jobs it provides, to another locality.

Another solution may come as a result of the rage that so many people feel when they learn how much water pollution is caused by the cynically selfish. This rage may turn against the companies who are doing the polluting and result in boycotts of their products. In the next few years more and more companies may find that it is good business to avoid all water pollution, even at a high cost, and to let their customers know that they are doing so.

Underground Wealth

Miners who rushed to Colorado in 1859 were too obsessed with their search for gold to think about preserving their essential water supply. Within a few months they had so muddied up the clear water of the mountain streams that their drinking water had to be packed in to them in barrels.

Since those days, miners all over the country have gone about their business with the same viewpoint, taking from the land its treasure of coal, iron, copper, uranium, gold, potash, salt, sulfur, oil, and other profitable minerals, and creating desolation and pollution along the way.

The cheapest method of gathering mineral deposits that lie close to the surface of the land is strip mining. In this process, all vegetation is cleared from the land, and then power shovels gouge out the ground containing the minerals. Strip mining leaves terrible scars on the face of the earth. The bare land is continually eroded by rain, which washes off sediment into streams and lakes. The runoff water picks up heavy acidity from the minerals on the ground and carries this pollution into the waterways.

Some state laws require that when miners have finished their work they restore the land again—replace the topsoil and vegetation to start the natural life cycles all over again. But this is a slow process and, so far, rehabilitation has been lagging far behind the destruction caused by strip mining.

Oil, one of the most valuable substances found under the ground, must be pumped up from pools within the earth's crust. In the early days of drilling for oil, particularly in Texas, some of the drilling bores went so deep that they tapped the briny water far inside the earth. This salty liquid came gushing up with the oil and spilled all over the land, killing the grass and the trees. Oil companies tried to drain the brine off into evaporation pits,

Strip mining is the cheapest method of taking minerals from the ground. It also is one of the greatest threats to the nation's water.

but many times heavy rain caused these to overflow. Then the brine seeped into the ground and ran into streams to such an extent that private wells were ruined and municipal water supplies were damaged. For a time, the Pecos River, which drains many of the Texas oil fields, was saltier than the ocean.

Modern and responsible oil companies now collect the brine as it comes to the surface and pump it back deep into the earth, far below the level of the underground reservoirs. This is an effective method of preserving the purity of the water supply. But so far no governing body has been able to police the oil fields effectively to make sure that all companies work in this way.

By whatever method they are mined, minerals come out of the earth mixed with impurities that have to be separated out and disposed of. These wastes are known as *tailings*. Sometimes they stand around mining areas in huge piles, blowing in the wind, and washing away with the runoff from rainstorms. Sometimes they are piped directly into nearby rivers or lakes. The piles of tailings at the uranium mines in Colorado and other Western states contain radioactive substances that are washed out by rain into the Platte River and other rivers in that part of the country.

In Minnesota, the state Pollution Control Agency and several citizens' groups have spent many years attempting to stop the Reserve Mining Company from pouring into Lake Superior the tailings from its taconite mining operation. Taconite is a rock that contains specks of iron. After it is mined, it is crushed and ground into small pieces. The iron-bearing particles are removed with a magnet, and the waste dust is washed away. Since Reserve Mining's plant went into operation in 1956, more than 190 million tons of taconite tailings have been put into the lake. Each day some 700 million gallons of water containing 67,000 tons of solid waste are pumped into Lake Superior. That tonnage is the equivalent of nearly 25,000 standard-sized automobiles.

The effect of these tailings upon Lake Superior has been a matter of dispute. The Pollution Control Agency contends that the water contains aluminum, lead, copper, zinc, cadmium, and nickel in concentrations that are dangerous to the natural life of the lake. They also cite evidence that the shrimp in the lake, which are an important

Until 1971, nearly a ton of taconite tailings entered the waters of Lake Superior each second.

source of food for the trout, smelt, and whitefish, are being affected. Lake trout and lake herring lay their eggs on the bottom of the lake, where they remain for a long incubation period. Some scientists say that the sediment from the taconite tailings is preventing many of the eggs from hatching. They also point out that the waters of Lake Superior are becoming cloudy, which keeps the sunlight from penetrating the lake's great depths. As a result, plants are unable to complete the process of photosynthesis and do their part in maintaining the other life in the lake. The tailings that are so heavily concentrated around the Reserve Mining plant have also been found in the water 50 miles away.

On the other hand, the Reserve Mining Company claims that the tailings have not significantly harmed the life within the lake or the quality of the water for drinking. And the company also says that continued dumping of tailings does not represent any greater hazard.

The Minnesota Pollution Control Agency, MECCA (Minnesota Environmental Control Citizens' Association), the Save Lake Superior Association, and the Sierra Club combined their efforts in an attempt to stop the dumping of tailings. Many public hearings and court cases resulted. In 1970 a Minnesota district court ruled in favor of Reserve Mining, saying that the PCA had not proved the tailings had an adverse effect on life within the lake. However, the court gave the company six months to develop a plan for changing its disposal method. When the time expired, the Environmental Protection Agency (EPA) and Reserve Mining had not agreed on an alternate method of disposal, and the EPA brought suit against the mining company. It remains to be seen whether or not Minnesota citizens will be able to save the waters of Lake Superior.

In a ruling in favor of the citizens' associations at an earlier hearing, Judge Donald Barbeau said, "If environmental quality is now of such major concern that the public will demand, and will sue for, strict enforcement of anti-pollution laws, the Court views that as a salutary development. The grim warnings of the ecologists that if we continue raping the land, befouling the water, and polluting the air, mankind itself will surely perish are barren admonitions unless they can be fortified by legal sanctions."

Riches under the Sea Bed

For many years geologists have known that rich deposits of oil and minerals lie under the sea bed, at the bottom of the oceans that cover 71 percent of the earth. The advanced technology of the 1960s made it possible to start mining these riches on a large scale, and companies all over the world are going ahead rapidly, without waiting to find out what damage they may be doing to life in the oceans.

Industrialists are not the only people who are rushing to mine the oceans. The American Museum of Natural History, a leader in the conservation movement, discovered deposits of a nearly pure form of calcium carbonate called aragonite on the sea bottom in the Bahamas. The institution was granted rights by the Bahamian government to mine the aragonite, and it encouraged the development, hoping it would provide an income. Later the museum sold its share of the stock for about $50,000. Unfortunately, no studies were made to find out if the mining would damage the life of the ocean.

Damage has been caused time and time again as a result of accidents in drilling for oil beneath the ocean floor. An oil well operated on a federal lease by the Union Oil Company in the Santa Barbara Channel blew out in January of 1969. It spilled a quarter of a million gallons of crude oil off the California coast. Ten days passed before the blowout was capped and sealed, and then pressures built up so that oil began to seep out through fissures in the ocean floor. Oil was washed ashore, smothering Santa

A murre (a common sea bird) who was a victim of the Santa Barbara oil slick

Two of the workboats used in the Santa Barbara clean-up. In the background, workmen are collecting oil-soaked hay into barrels.

Barbara's resort beaches and coating the rocks of the offshore islands—the home of seals, sea lions, and sea birds. At least 1,200 sea birds were killed. Sea lion pups starved after being abandoned by their mothers; the oil they had wriggled over camouflaged their own distinctive scent so that their mothers could not recognize them.

The oil company provided clean-up crews who went to work on the beaches, blotting up the oil with truckloads of hay and steam-cleaning the overhanging rocks. But even when the sand again looked clean, a heavy footprint, a sandpile on the beach, or a rough storm revealed the black muck lurking just below the surface.

Angry residents in the area set up an organization called GOO (Get Oil Out). Santa Barbara citizens, city council members, and county board supervisors believed almost unanimously that the offshore drilling must stop. Many lawsuits were filed against the oil company to collect for the terrific amount of damage the oil had caused. But Congress showed little interest in supporting a proposed bill to halt the drilling, and within a year the Department of the Interior and the United States Army Corps of Engineers granted new leases to the Humble Oil Company for drilling more oil wells in the Santa Barbara Channel.

Louisiana, too, has suffered pollution of its ocean and coastline from offshore drilling. In March 1970 three wells belonging to Chevron Oil blew out. Together they spewed 600 to 1,000 barrels of crude oil a day into the Gulf of Mexico, creating a 26-mile-long oil slick that threatened the gulf's oyster beds, shrimp grounds, and bird havens.

After the Santa Barbara oil spill, an old regulation had been reinforced; offshore wells were supposed to be fitted with storm choke safety devices that shut off the oil flow when there is a sudden change of pressure. Inspection after the Louisiana oil spill showed that 137 of Chevron's 178 wells did *not* have these storm chokes in operation. Chevron was fined $1 million for failure to comply with the regulation.

A panel of experts reported to the President in 1969 that by 1980 the United States could expect an oil pollution disaster once a year unless offshore blowouts could be controlled. The panel also pointed out that there have been blowouts in 25 of the approximately 8,000 offshore wells that have been drilled since 1954. In the 25 blowouts, 17 leaked gas only, 2 caused serious pollution incidents, and 9 caused deaths as a result of fire.

A burning well off the coast of Louisiana, March 1970. Thousands of barrels of oil leaked into the Gulf of Mexico.

On the High Seas

On March 18, 1967, the *Torrey Canyon* was wrecked on the Seven Stones Reef, 30 miles off the southwest tip of England. Many ships had been wrecked there before, but this time the disaster was especially serious. The ship was a tanker carrying over 100,000 tons of crude oil in her 16 cargo tanks —enough oil to supply 660,180 American-sized automobiles with gasoline for one month.

The *Torrey Canyon*, a modern ship with every aid to navigation, hit a well-charted rock in a calm sea. Some of its tanks were immediately ruptured and began spilling their oil into the ocean. Other tanks remained intact. At first it was hoped that the ship could be refloated and towed to port, where the oil could be pumped out. But soon a storm came in. The sea grew too rough for rescue operations to begin, and the ship settled harder onto the rocks. She began pounding against the reef, opening up more of her tanks.

The oil gushed out, killing marine life for hundreds of miles. It spread an evil-smelling black sludge over the beautiful beaches of Cornwall, in England, and Brittany, in France, destroying their tourist trade for that year. Twenty-five coastal villages in France were declared

Oil on a beach in France after the *Torrey Canyon* broke up near the English coast

devastated areas. More than 25,000 birds were killed by the oil. Mussel and oyster farms, which had been built up over many years, were destroyed. Fishermen lost their livelihood because markets would not accept their polluted catches. French naval air observers spotted an oil slick over 60 miles long being propelled out into the Atlantic Ocean by northeast winds.

The *Torrey Canyon* was carrying 118,000 tons of oil for the Union Oil Company of California. Today there are tankers being planned to carry twice that amount. In 1970, about 5,000 tankers were afloat, together carrying 700 million tons of crude oil. Even without accidents, most tankers cause some pollution; they wash out their tanks with sea water, discharging the dirty water back into the ocean—despite international agreements that this will not be done. At least once a year a tanker somewhere runs aground and spills its cargo. Oil-carrying barges break up in collisions. Mysterious oil slicks appear where no accidents are known to have happened. By now these incidents are hardly even considered news. But steadily and increasingly, oil is contaminating ocean waters, destroying marine life, and desecrating the beaches of the world.

Passenger liners and freighters are another source of pollution in the ocean. Sometimes they fill their empty fuel tanks with water for ballast and then pump this highly contaminated mixture overboard before entering port. They also discharge their untreated sewage and garbage directly into the ocean.

The oceans are used as garbage dumps by landlubbers too. Garbage from New York City is daily towed out to sea and dropped into the water, sometimes turning up ashore again as far away as Virginia. Nerve gas has been dumped in the ocean off the coast of Florida and in the North Sea. Governments all over the world dispose of concrete canisters containing radioactive wastes by dropping them into the ocean. On occasion the pressure at great depths causes these canisters to implode, and their highly dangerous wastes are scattered with the tides. Off the coast of California, canisters dumped by the Atomic Energy Commission imploded, and fish caught two hours later were showing abnormal levels of strontium 90, a radioactive isotope highly dangerous to man.

As mentioned earlier, pesticides that are washed off the land into rivers and lakes are eventually carried into the oceans. Other chemicals, of many kinds, have leaked into river estuaries and oceans from barges damaged in collisions. Some biologists estimate that all the food life in the world's oceans will be destroyed within 50 years if men maintain their present levels of pollution. Moreover, there is a real danger of destroying the oceanic plant life, which produces about 60 percent of the world's newly released oxygen each year.

When the explorer Thor Heyerdahl was crossing the Atlantic in his papyrus raft, he saw plastic bottles and other debris floating in the water far away from any land. At one point, the ocean water was so filthy that he and his companions could not use it for washing. During a second trip Heyerdahl radioed to the United Nations: "At least a continuous stretch of 1,400 miles of the open Atlantic is polluted by floating lumps of solidified, asphalt-like oil."

Man-made Waterways

Private industry is not the only contributor to the damage to American waterways; the federal government also must take some of the blame. Many a Congressman has gone proudly back to his home state, confident of increased popularity —and therefore increased votes— because he has secured federal support for an irrigation project or a water transport plan to be carried out by the Army Corps of Engineers or the Bureau of Reclamation. The use of local contractors and equipment, he reports to his constituents, will be a substantial boon to the state's economy. However, not many of the citizens realize what the project may do to their waterways.

Most of the man-made waterway schemes do not directly pollute the water; they do not add sewage or chemicals or heat to lakes and rivers. But like the dams for hydroelectric power plants, they destroy areas of natural beauty. Most of them also change the wildlife of the area by eliminating its natural habitat and creating an environment that does not supply the food and cover required by the creatures which have been living there. Moreover, there seems to be very little reason for doing many of these projects, except for the construction revenues they provide.

Minnesota, for example, built an involved system of dams, locks, and dredged channels at St. Anthony Falls on the Mississippi River in Minneapolis. This project took $30.3 million of federal money and was supposed to aid commercial river traffic up river from the city. However, this traffic is nearly nonexistent.

The Oklawaha barge canal scheme in Florida also seemed to be expensive and unnecessary. However, it took on a more sinister implication; it was destroying an area of great beauty, one that was the home of many kinds of wildlife, including alligator, heron, wild turkey,

The Obion River in Tennessee. The Army Corps of Engineers has channeled the stream to drain the surrounding wetlands, producing additional areas of cropland. However, a life system that includes duck, fish, raccoon, squirrel, and deer is being destroyed.

black bear, and panther. Estimates of the cost of the canal made in 1950 were $164 million, but by 1970 the estimates had risen to between $180 million and $210 million. Yet it was likely that by 1990 the canal would have carried tonnage equivalent to only one 100-car freight train.

Well-organized business groups, developers, trade associations, and political lobbyists who supported the plan said that the Oklawaha barge canal would provide jobs for pilots, tug operators, line handlers, insurers, bankers, shipyard workers, shipping agents, freight handlers, and so on. Conservationists, on the other hand, saw the project as a piece of unnecessary development for private profit.

One-half of the crucial 33-mile stretch of the Oklawaha River was destroyed; a dam was built and a reservoir was formed. Then conservationists went to court in an attempt to prevent the rest of the project from going through. In June 1970 the Secretary of the Interior set up a special task force to study the effects of the canal on the ecology of the area and asked the Army Corps of Engineers to delay the work for 15 months while the studies were made. Finally, in January 1971, President Nixon, acting on the recommendation of the Council on Environmental Quality, ordered work on the canal to cease.

The California Water Project is another Corps project under attack from conservationists. This is a state-long system of reservoirs, dams, canals, aqueducts, pipelines, and pumping stations that will carry fresh water from northern California to the dry lands of southern California. Further plans are projected to connect other rivers to this system, drawing on those in Oregon, Washington, Canada, and even Alaska.

The Corps of Engineers, the state Department of Water Resources, Governor Ronald Reagan, California bankers and land developers, and others in favor of the project say that it will take the "surplus" water that flows to the ocean through San Francisco Bay and use it for agricultural, municipal, and industrial development farther south. Conservationists object that this will destroy the free-flowing wild rivers of the north. They also point out

A drawing of the California State Water Project. No one knows how this project will affect life systems in the state.

that the project will turn the San Francisco Bay delta, which now supports over a million water birds, into a brackish cesspool.

The Egyptians are beginning to learn what can happen when man alters the balances of natural water systems. The huge Aswan Dam has realized man's centuries-old ambition of harnessing and controlling the waters of the Nile River. Farmers of the Nile valley are no longer at the mercy of floods and droughts, and 1.2 million acres of land have been added to the country's farming area. But the dam holds back the rich silt that formerly came down with the annual flood waters and remained in the soil when the floods ran off. Thus the fertility of the farmers' lands is slowly being decreased. Lack of this silt, and the nutrition it contains, has also damaged marine life in the eastern Mediterranean, so that the sardine fishermen find they are getting smaller catches.

3

True Murder Stories

So Long, Lake Erie

The killing of Lake Erie is a mob job—the combined efforts of some 11 million people who live near its shores and along the rivers and tributaries that empty into it. They are being aided and abetted by 360 industrial companies that discharge their wastes into the water.

Nine million people in the area are served by sewers and sewage treatment plants. But more than half of the plants give only primary treatment; that is, they strain out the solids and sludge, and then pump out the rest of the liquid without further treatment into the nearest waterway. Two million people live without sewers at all and discharge their raw wastes directly into the rivers and the lake. Thus sewage is one of the main sources of pollution in Lake Erie.

Giant industries, including household names like Ford,

Bethlehem Steel, Gulf Oil, and Hammermill Paper, discharge 9.6 billion gallons of water a day into the lake and its rivers, much of it contaminated with dangerous and filthy pollutants. These include acids, oil, cyanide, iron, phenol, and toxic metals such as copper, cadmium, chromium, lead, nickel, zinc, and iron. Poisonous chemicals enter the water from pesticides off agricultural land and from plastics and chemical industries. Phosphates pour in from fertilizers and detergents.

Also, power plants contribute thermal pollution to the water. And the radioactive content of the lake is rising, partly from the increasing numbers of atomic power plants being built along the shores.

Other pollutants in the lake include oily wastes, fish entrails, and human excrement from commercial and pleasure boats. In addition, spoil from harbor dredging— 6 million cubic yards each year—is dumped into the middle of the lake. Soil particles picked up from eroded land areas and from highway and urban development also clog the water. Trash and debris are widespread at all depths of the lake.

All of these pollutants have varied effects on Lake Erie. Some use up the oxygen in the water when they decay. Others overstimulate the growth of underwater plants, leading to accelerated eutrophication, so that even more oxygen is lost. Some pollutants are poisonous, killing plant life, microorganisms, and the fish that feed upon them. And the decay of all this matter causes even more decomposition and loss of oxygen. Other pollutants color and obscure the water so that the sunlight cannot get through, causing the death of organisms that depend on sunlight. The inevitable result, if the pollution of Lake

A beach on Lake Erie, near the city of Detroit

Erie continues, is a dead lake—water that is of no value to man or animal.

Eighty-seven beaches on Lake Erie were closed down by 1968. Commercial and sport fishing declined disastrously, and now there are restrictions on the sale of fish caught in Lake Erie because they are so contaminated. Some species of fish have disappeared altogether. Ships are prohibited by the Public Health Service from taking drinking water out of the lake unless they are equipped to give it full cleansing treatment. In Cleveland, the inadequate sewage treatment system is allowing raw sewage to contaminate the residents' own drinking water. A doctor in the area made tests which showed that there were dangerous germs in water that had sat in the pipes overnight. He regularly treats patients for vomiting and

Cleveland, Ohio. The Cuyahoga River empties its load of pollutants (light in color) into the darker waters of Lake Erie.

diarrhea after they have drunk water or eaten food out of the lake.

Erie is a tough little lake. Because it receives a high volume of good quality water from Lake Huron and empties out vigorously over Niagara Falls, it has a rapid *flush-out time*. This helps to replace the polluted water with cleaner water. But the attacks upon Lake Erie are now so strong and so unceasing that little hope remains for its survival.

The forces of law and conservation are making rumbling noises, threatening to take action against the industries and cities that are the major polluters. But they are going to have to move fast, enforce the spending of vast amounts of money, and do a major clean-up in record time if Lake Erie is to be saved.

In 1970 federal investigators reported that most cities and some industries were falling far behind pledges they had made earlier to clean the water that flows into Lake Erie. The federal government also was accused of failing to provide the money it had promised and of failing to clean the waste waters under its own control.

The River that Burst into Flames

Nobody knows what sparked off the fire. Perhaps it was a lighted cigarette thrown from a barge or a bridge; perhaps a match, still flaring as it hit the water. But on Monday, July 7, 1969, flames licked the surface of the Cuyahoga River in Cleveland, Ohio. Instead of being quenched by the water, the flames spread. Soon a whole section of the river was blazing. Two railroad bridges less than a mile from the center of Cleveland caught fire. The steel rails on both bridges warped and curled in the heat.

75

The Cuyahoga River aflame. This body of water has the unusual distinction of being a fire hazard.

A river tug was trapped in the flames. By the time fire trucks and a fireboat had the blaze under control, $50,000 worth of damage had been done.

It was not, of course, the water itself that burned. The flames fed on the wastes that have been spewed out into the Cuyahoga for years. The choking debris of oil, scum, sewage, garbage, and industrial wastes provide a perpetual fire hazard, especially when combined with the foul-smelling gases that can be seen rising from the river.

The once-beautiful Cuyahoga flows southwest along the eastern edge of the Cleveland metropolitan area, enters the city of Akron, and then turns north into Cleveland's industrial center. Finally it empties into Lake Erie. By the time it reaches the lake, it is chocolate brown with patches of dark red, and in some areas it is every color of the rainbow. At this stage the Cuyahoga carries no visible underwater life—not even the low forms like leeches and sludge-worms that usually thrive on waste.

The sources of pollution are many. All along its route the Cuyahoga is used as an open sewer by the communities on its banks. Half-treated and raw sewage, organic sludge, and decomposing algae rot in its waters, carrying disease-ridden organisms downstream to the next community. The city of Cleveland is one of the major sewage polluters.

Several steel companies, including Republic Steel, U.S. Steel, and Jones & Laughlin, discharge iron particles, oil, sulphates, ammonia, acids, scums, sludge, and other life-destroying wastes into the Cuyahoga. Harshaw Chemical flushes out into the river solid wastes, nickel, fluorides, other chemicals, and acids. Sonoco Oil Products adds a reddish tinge to the water. Downriver from the Firestone, Goodrich, and Goodyear tire companies and from Diamond Salt, the water is warm, dark, and murky, has a strong odor, is thick with oils and complex organic wastes, and is poisoned by chlorides.

After the July 1969 fire, the mayor of Cleveland pleaded with the Ohio state government to stop issuing waste-dumping permits for industries along the Cuyahoga. But there was no immediate response. On any day at all, the river could burn again.

Violence along the Mississippi

Old Man River flows through the heartland of the United States. Together with over 250 tributaries, it drains more than 40 percent of the entire country. At the peak of the spring floods, the river pours over 2 million cubic feet of water every second into the Gulf of Mexico, sometimes carrying whole houses and barns on its racing tide. It sweeps along 350 million cubic yards of mud, sand, gravel, and silt each year, depositing some of it on the shores of the gulf and taking the rest out to sea.

Farther up river, dams and turbines harness the current, and there is a busy traffic of tugs and barges, sometimes in strings more than 1,000 feet long. The barges carry oil, coal, cotton, steel, and many other products of the cities along the river.

At the source of the Mississippi in northern Minnesota a man can straddle the stream and freely drink its cool, clear water. At the Gulf of Mexico, 2,470 miles away, the Mississippi has carved itself an extensive delta on the shore, and the main channel is more than a mile wide. At this point no sensible person would drink, or even swim in, the water which has become fouled with the pollution of nearly half the nation.

Around 1900, Mark Twain wrote of the "magnificent Mississippi, rolling its mile-wide tide along, shining in the sun." Today, pollution experts describe that same river as the "colon of mid-America."

For years a slovenly society has been inflicting on the river all its insults and indignities. Hundreds of towns and cities use the Mississippi as a sewer, some unloading their sewage without any treatment at all, others giving it only primary treatment. "Every time you take a glass of water from a faucet in St. Louis," said Richard Amberg, publisher of that city's *Globe-Democrat*, "you are drinking from every flush toilet from here to Minnesota." Only a few responsible communities clean their effluent properly before discharging the water into the river.

Thousands of manufacturing plants, stockyards, packing plants, refineries, and paper mills drain their wastes into the Mississippi. The pollutants include phenols, toxic metals, oils, chicken feathers, garbage, radioactive waste, chemical sludge, and raw blood from the slaughterhouses. For long stretches of miles at a time, the water is so robbed of its oxygen that none of its living creatures can survive. Fish and water birds are killed. Spawning beds (where fish lay their eggs) are smothered by oil, silt, and sludge.

Endrin, dieldrin, DDT, and other pesticides are washed into the river in the runoff from agricultural lands. In the early 1960s, concentrations of endrin were so high that a government investigation was ordered. Large amounts of endrin were found in the bottom of a sewer near the Memphis plant of Velsicol, a company that manufactures the pesticide. As soon as this was discovered, Velsicol took immediate steps to seal off and bypass the sewer and to install new controls. But the use of pesticides continues in the farmlands drained by the Mississippi River, and most of the chemicals eventually enter the water.

The river is also polluted by the traffic it carries. Barges have accidents from time to time, spilling their cargoes into the water. One, damaged when it collided with a wharf and then with a towboat near New Orleans, leaked 1,600 barrels of crude oil into the Mississippi. Immediately a New Orleans suburb was forced to cut off its

79

supply of river water and switch to a small emergency reservoir, sufficient to supply its needs for only a few hours. Fortunately for the community (but not for the waters of the earth) the oil was carried along by a swift current and within one day had traveled more than a hundred miles to the mouth of the river, where it was disgorged into the Gulf of Mexico.

The attacks made on the Mississippi are no secret. Yet, so far, the sheer size of the problem has kept it from being solved. Nine different states line the river's banks, many with their own water pollution control agencies. The federal government also has authority over the Mississippi because it is an interstate waterway. And each city and county along the way has its own needs and responsibilities. Every tributary running into the Mississippi contributes its own share of pollution. United and massive efforts to clean up this, the greatest of the nation's rivers, are urgently needed.

Red Means Dead in the Gulf of Mexico

There is a red menace off the coast of Florida that has nothing to do with communism. Every now and again the ocean turns red. Fish start leaping about in a frenzy. Gradually, as the activity subsides, one fish after another floats belly up, dead. Thousands of dead fish get washed ashore to rot on Florida's beaches, and they have to be shoved by municipal bulldozers into lime-filled pits.

This occurrence is known as the red tide. It has been observed throughout the world, but it seems to be getting more and more frequent off Florida's western coast, an area which is especially rich in oysters, fish, sea birds, turtles, and other marine life. The red tide was observed there in 1916, then in 1932. The next appearance was in 1946, but in that year it stayed around for 10 months and killed about 50 million fish. The effects on sport fishing, commercial fishing, and tourism were so disastrous that dozens of inquiries and scientific investigations were set up.

Marine biologists discovered that the killer was an organism named *Gymnodium breve*—nicknamed Jim Brevis—a kind of whirling plankton with whiplike appendages, measuring only one-thousandth of an inch across. These plankton are natural organisms, half plant, half animal, which drift like a cloud in the sea and provide good feeding for fish and whales.

In normal times there are about a thousand Jim Brevis in a quart of ocean water. But when a red tide occurs, something—and after years of study no one knows for sure just what—triggers a fantastic population explosion until suddenly there are 60 million Jim Brevis per quart, staining the sea red. Some kinds of plankton, when they bloom like this, provide rich food for the fish. But when Jim Brevis blooms it excretes a waste that immobilizes the nervous system of fish, causing convulsions, then death. Even the chemical warfare branch of the army has so far failed to isolate and identify the toxin.

After the red tide went away in 1947, concern gradually died down. A government laboratory studying blooms of Jim Brevis was even closed down for the sake of economy. But then, in 1953, the sea off Fort Myers turned red. It turned again in 1954. Then the red tide skipped a couple of years, but it has occurred somewhere on the Florida gulf coast every year since 1957.

Researchers have found that some outbreaks of red tide

Dead fish float in the water off the coast of Florida. They were killed by an invasion of the red tide.

coincide with periods of heavy rainfall, when the rivers discharge nearly twice their normal amount of water into the gulf. Various pollutants from the rivers have been tested as possible "trigger mechanisms" for the blooming of Jim Brevis, but none has yet proved to be the cause. Copper sulfate crystals dropped on the red patches kill the toxic plankton, but only temporarily. Within a week the organisms reappear, as deadly as ever.

People can swim in the red tide without harm. But serious cases of poisoning from shellfish have been linked to the toxins of the red tide. No one knows whether the phenomenon will continue to appear more and more often off the Florida gulf coast, or whether it will again die away as part of a cycle that man does not understand.

But in the meantime the red tide is casting a blight on Florida's vacationland. It is yet another pollutant in the waters of the Gulf of Mexico—in addition to oil spills, dumped nerve gas, sewage from ships and shore, and the many wastes swirling into the gulf from the Mississippi River.

Poison Creeps up on the Columbia River

Up in Canada the Columbia is a wild and joyful river. It cascades recklessly over rocks and boulders, goes flashing down the mountain valleys. As the river crosses the United States border it begins to sober up, its free flow interrupted by the huge Grand Coulee Dam in the state of Washington. Below the dam, with the current regulated by man, it becomes a grand and beautiful river, passing through magnificent scenery. It is a paradise for water sports and vacations.

But near the southern part of Washington, there is a 50-mile stretch of the Columbia River that is closed to the public. Boats may travel this reach by special permission only, and then usually accompanied by an official escort. In this area full military security is maintained for the Hanford works of the Atomic Energy Commission.

This is the largest diffusion plant in the world; it is here that much of the nation's uranium is purified. In the past, Hanford also produced plutonium in its large reactors. The reactors were cooled by river water which was then discharged back into the Columbia at a temperature of 95 degrees, with all its known hazards of thermal pollution. In addition, radioactive wastes leaked out or were discharged into the air and into the water.

Unfortunately, when plutonium production at Hanford ceased in 1971, radioactive pollution did not. In this same area is a giant graveyard for the storage of high-level radioactive wastes, produced as a result of the work done in the Hanford plant and in the nuclear industry in other parts of the country. The wastes are concentrated and then stored in million-gallon tanks of stainless steel and concrete, where they have to be cooled, watched, and maintained for thousands of years. They generate their own immense heat, so that large cooling equipment is

Part of the Atomic Energy Commission's Hanford works

needed inside each tank to hold the temperature down to a manageable 700 degrees. The wastes are so toxic that they gradually erode even the toughest tanks yet devised.

Monitoring instruments surround the tanks to detect the beginnings of any leakage. When leaks occur the waste has to be pumped out of the old tank and into a new one.

The tanks are set into the ground and, to keep a check on leakage from them, the Atomic Energy Commission has drilled test wells all around the site. The tests show that some of the radioactive waste has leaked as far as 18 miles underground, and some has escaped into the Columbia River. No one will reveal how much waste there is, although it is estimated at over 100 million gallons. The exact amount is a closely guarded secret because any figures on the waste being stored might enable scientists to calculate the volume of weapons being made. No one will reveal, either, how much radioactive waste has so far contaminated the river.

Tests have been made by an independent research organization to check the levels of radioactivity in the bodies of people who live in the Pasco-Kennewick area (just downstream from the AEC reservation), who work at the Hanford plant, and who have farms in the area. It is hoped that the results will be published, so that the public can know what the findings were. Earlier research, some time ago, showed that residents in the area carried in their bodies more radioactive material than is usually absorbed from a natural background.

As the Columbia River flows on, leaving this sinister area behind, it reaches the Oregon border and turns westward to come eventually to the Pacific Ocean. Along the way, it provides water supplies for the cities on its banks, including the busy areas of Vancouver and Portland. So far no one knows what the cumulative effects may be from the invisible poisons lurking in the water.

4

The Way Ahead

It is difficult to believe that man, a creature with enough intelligence and technological skill to make a controlled environment so that he can walk for hours on the airless, waterless moon, is the same creature who is wantonly destroying his own natural environment here on earth. Yet this is what is happening. Scientists have been sounding the warning for years, but only in the late 1960s did the message start getting through to the general public: the environment, and therefore the existence of man himself, is in danger. Perhaps the warning has been heeded just in time. But action must be taken quickly.

The waters of the earth cannot hold out much longer. It is clear that the demand for water will continue to increase, as the population grows and as technology advances. Many scientists believe that within 10 years so little clean water will be left that water rationing will have to be imposed in the United States. And with so much pollution at sea, it is no longer possible to expect the riches of the ocean to feed the coming population. Nor is it possible to feel confident that ocean plants will continue to renew more than half of the world's oxygen, as they do now.

In the past, man has rampaged over the earth, congratulating himself on his success in conquering nature, in bending it to his own needs. He has been so pleased with his own cleverness, with his own ingenuity in making such intricate things as rocket ships and stereo sets, that he has forgotten he is just one small part of the web of life on earth. He has made prosperity the measure of his success, without realizing that prosperity run wild could cost him life itself.

If the waters of the earth are polluted until they can no longer support life, then the earth will lose the supply of oxygen that keeps all creatures alive. That is how dependent man is on the web of life. All the citizens of the world are going to need a drastic change of heart, so that they treat the balance of nature with a new respect and no longer destroy the world either because they are too ignorant to realize what is happening or because they shut their ears to the truth when they find it uncomfortable.

Now that researchers have learned so much about the chemistry of the intricate checks and balances of the natural life cycles of the earth, men must insist that careful tests are made before anyone tampers with the water, the air, or the land. Before scooping up the bed of the ocean by the ton, they must experiment to see how this will affect the life of the ocean and therefore all living things. Before drilling for oil through the Alaskan permafrost, men must find out what this will do to the land—an area that has remained unchanged since the ice age and is part of the Arctic, whose frozen wastes help control the temperature of the whole world. Before obliterating some disease-carrying insect with a new wonder chemical, they must study the effect this will have on the various food chains of which the insect forms a part, and also what side effects the chemical will have on other living things. Everyone must develop a healthy suspicion of new actions that are likely to affect the environment.

To take effective action, it is necessary to learn to seek out the facts. No longer can anyone avoid the issues because they seem too confused, too difficult. The people in charge of the news media must be convinced that their readers and listeners want full information, honestly stated, and that they are prepared to make the effort of concentration required to understand this information.

Concerned citizens must learn to use democratic processes of government, so that Senators and Representatives realize that the views of the men and women who elect them are more important than the pressures of the industrial lobbies. The Congressmen must know that if they fail to respond to those views, they will forfeit the goodwill, and therefore the votes, of their electorate.

It is also necessary to learn to make difficult decisions. When a major industry in a city protests at being asked to curb the pollution it is causing, and then threatens to close down the plant and move elsewhere, a basic conflict arises. The fear of unemployment is closer to home than the fear of destroying life on earth. A just decision can be made only when the facts are known—the facts as they relate to the whole world, not just to one community.

When pollution control regulations are equally stringent and enforced with equal vigor all over the United States, then industrialists will not be able to blackmail a single community in this manner.

There is no way to avoid the fact that water pollution control costs money. It may mean higher taxes. It may mean increased production costs for many industries. In one way or another these costs must be borne by the taxpayer and the consumer—by the whole society. But these costs are small compared to the destructive costs of uncontrolled pollution, and small compared to the costs of running out of clean water.

Through the spread of information and knowledge, a climate of opinion must be created in which no self-respecting businessman or municipality will pollute the environment of any area. Effective laws are necessary to force the hands of businesses and communities without self-respect, and those laws must be enforced.

It is important for those who are working to fight pollution to concentrate their energies. Several conservation societies banded together will be more effective than separate ones acting independently of each other. For years government action against pollution was handicapped because there were 92 different agencies involved. Now a federal Environmental Protection Agency has been established, providing for more effective action by concentrating the responsibility within one office.

Rhetoric and emotional outbursts are not enough. They are useful to shock people into understanding the seriousness of the damage being done to the waters of the earth. But the clean-up will take years to accomplish. It will be necessary to use facts and information to provide a basic motivation—to be sure that the enthusiasm does not run out before the job is done. Only an educated public can push government and industry into action.

Each of us can begin now, in our day-to-day lives, to help protect the waters of the earth. Be stingy with electricity—remember the water pollution that results from every kilowatt produced. Measure out detergent carefully and choose those brands that contain little or no phosphates. Avoid chemical fertilizers and weed killers. Don't use near water those containing phosphates. Find out where the sewage goes from your home or school. Does it get adequate treatment? Where is the water finally discharged? And does it cause pollution there? Join the local conservation society. Ask them what can be done to help fight the special problems in your local area. When you see pollution, make a fuss. Write to the newspapers, to television and radio stations, to your Congressman. Contact the local authorities in charge of water pollution control. Get your family, friends, and neighbors to join in.

However, even following all these guidelines is not enough; it does not earn us the luxury of sitting back comfortably and thinking, "Well, I've done my share." The pollution of years past threatens everyone. For a long time no one understood just how much damage was being done. But now the facts are clear. They must be believed. And we must make drastic efforts to put things right. Time is no longer on our side. Young people living today are the first generation to know that every act of pollution will threaten the lives of their own children.

During all the millions of years that man has been developing, the other creatures of the world have been evolving beside him, along their separate evolutionary

A hopeful sign on the Mad River in Ohio

chains. Some did not make it because they could not adapt to changes in climate and food supply, or perhaps because they could not escape from other creatures that were hunting them for food. The dinosaur, for example, died out, as did the dodo bird, the mammoth, and many, many more. So far, man as a species has survived, at least for something like 2 million years. But the beginnings of life on earth go back for billions of years. This means that we have existed for only about one-millionth of that time, and we have no guarantee that we will prove any more durable than some of the other creatures that have become extinct. Now we are faced with the enormous problem of pollution, and this might possibly turn out to be a major change in the environment that we cannot survive.

The next few years will show whether we are prepared to use the same energy and invention to stay alive that we have used to build industrial complexes or to get to the moon.

Glossary

biodegradables. Materials that can be decomposed by natural, organic processes.

biological amplification. The accumulation of a substance in greater and greater concentrations as it moves up a food chain.

biota. The interrelated organisms that make up the "life" of a particular body of water or region.

effluent. The outflow of water from a particular source, such as a building or a sewage treatment plant.

eutrophication. The natural aging process of a body of water. Over many thousands of years, a lake will become a swamp and finally a meadow. Adding nutrients from sewage, fertilizers, and detergents can greatly accelerate eutrophication.

flush-out time. The length of time required for the water in a lake to flow out and be replaced with new water.

food chain. A system of interrelated organisms in a body of water or a region. Each intermediate link in the chain feeds on the organisms below it and is itself food for the organisms above it.

half-life. The length of time required for half the atoms of a radioactive substance to break down and disintegrate. Also, the time it takes half the molecules in a chemical compound to break down into separate elements.

hydrological cycle. The process of evaporation and precipitation that constantly recirculates the waters of the earth. Water moves from the oceans to the air, to the land, and back to the oceans.

nonbiodegradables. Inorganic substances that cannot be broken down by normal environmental processes.

phosphates. Compounds derived from phosphoric acid, used in detergents and fertilizers. They may be one of the major causes of excessive algae growth in freshwater lakes.

photosynthesis. The process by which green plants manufacture food. Light energy combines with carbon dioxide, water, and inorganic salts to produce carbohydrates. When this happens, oxygen is released as a by-product.

plankton. Microscopic plant and animal organisms which live in fresh and salt water. They are a source of food for many fish, and they also supply oxygen to the atmosphere.

siltation. The addition of particles of mud and sand to a body of water, usually the result of erosion.

tailings. Impurities that remain after the valuable minerals are separated from ore.

thermal pollution. The addition of heat to a body of water, raising the temperature above normal conditions.

Index

About the Authors

Pollution: The Waters of the Earth is one of eight books on pollution written by Claire Jones, Steve J. Gadler, and Paul H. Engstrom. This volume was a cooperative effort, each person contributing his or her own knowledge and experience, with the final result a kind of "literary synergism."

Paul H. Engstrom is a minister, a lawyer, and a family counselor, as well as president and cofounder of the Minnesota Environmental Control Citizens' Association. Under his leadership, MECCA has worked for preservation of Lake Superior and the Mississippi watershed, reduction of radioactive pollution, reuse of materials in solid waste, and many other environmental goals to improve the quality of life. Thus Rev. Engstrom's major contribution to this series of books on pollution was a social and legal perspective resulting from direct experience.

Steve J. Gadler also is experienced in the fight to save the environment; he is a registered professional engineer who was an environmentalist long before pollution became a national issue. A retired Air Force Colonel, Mr. Gadler has for many years been asking pertinent, revealing questions about the damage caused by our industrial society. He has been especially concerned about radioactivity, which is an invisible but deadly threat to life itself. In 1967, the governor of Minnesota appointed him as a member of the state's Pollution Control Agency. Mr. Gadler's technical expertise is apparent in each book in the series.

Claire Jones is an experienced writer who first became aware of the dangers of pollution in 1956, when she lived through one of the famous London killer smogs. Teaming up with Rev. Engstrom and Mr. Gadler gave her an excellent way to express her concern over the condition of the environment. However, her contribution has been more than a concerned citizen's point of view and a crisp, sparkling writing style. A native of England, Mrs. Jones brings a special international outlook to this series. None of the problems of pollution can be seen as less than worldwide, and this important perspective gives *The Waters of the Earth* added value.